T0057550

Quickly Changing River

ALSO BY MEENA ALEXANDER

POETRY

Stone Roots

House of a Thousand Doors

The Storm: A Poem in Five Parts (chapbook)

Night-Scene, the Garden (chapbook)

River and Bridge

The Shock of Arrival: Reflections on Postcolonial Experience (poems and essays)

Illiterate Heart

Raw Silk

PROSE

Women in Romanticism: Mary Wollstonecraft, Dorothy Wordsworth, and Mary Shelley

Nampally Road

Fault Lines: A Memoir

Manhattan Music

MEENA ALEXANDER

Quickly Changing River

❧ *poems* ❧

TRIQUARTERLY BOOKS

NORTHWESTERN UNIVERSITY PRESS

EVANSTON, ILLINOIS

TriQuarterly Books
Northwestern University Press
www.nupress.northwestern.edu

Copyright © 2008 by Meena Alexander.
Published 2008 by Northwestern University Press. All rights reserved.

Printed in the United States of America

10 9 8 7 6 5 4 3 2 1

Library of Congress Cataloging-in-Publication Data

Alexander, Meena, 1951–
  Quickly changing river : poems / Meena Alexander.
    p. cm.
  Includes bibliographical references.
  ISBN-13: 978-0-8101-2450-9 (cloth : alk. paper)
  ISBN-10: 0-8101-2450-5 (cloth : alk. paper)
  ISBN-13: 978-0-8101-2451-6 (pbk. : alk. paper)
  ISBN-10: 0-8101-2451-3 (pbk. : alk. paper)
  I. Title.
PR9499.3.A46Q53 2008
811.54—dc22
                                              2007035885

∞ The paper used in this publication meets the minimum requirements
    of the American National Standard for Information Sciences—
Permanence of Paper for Printed Library Materials, ANSI Z39.48-1992.

For my mother

Can you cut water in two?
    —TALLAPAKA ANNAMACHARYA

The white wake left by the passage,
the quick tremulous whirl of the wheels,
The flags of all nations, the falling of them at sunset . . .
    —WALT WHITMAN

Contents

~

~

Quickly Changing River

COSMOPOLITAN

You want a poem on being cosmopolitan.
Dear friend, what can I say?

Sometimes I cannot tell mulberry skin
From blood on the hands of children.

Nor stop myself from tugging a cloth
Where ghostly knives, cups, forks flutter,

Where stones surrender to the hunger of exiles.
Yesterday I jumped the metal door confusing D train for A,

Doors clashed, I tore a sleeve, saved my arm.
Pacing the ill-lit platform

I heard the bird of heaven call.
A cry huge, indigo,

Bursting the underground tunnel.
A simple enough bird

Whose voice alone forces it apart.
A dun-colored thing, feathers moist

It likes best to perch on green tamarind
Or on a bamboo branch.

The kind of bird you see painted
On palmyra fans

Or at the rim of raw silk
Furnishing a woman's garment.

~

As the A train spun in, I saw claws
Scoring a stubble field,

Rails melting into bamboo hit by a lightning storm.
Ill suited for that train

And wherever in the world it might take me,
I set both hands to the tunnel wall.

In cracks of the broken wall I touched dirt, moist, reddening.
It came to me foolish perhaps,

Yet insistent as night wind after a storm has passed.
Slow, sweet tapping on the tympanum:

This is where your home is laid,
Scales unsung and secret geography.

~

Odd questions massed in me.
Who knows my name or where my skin was torn?
If I could would I return to Kashi?
And might the queen of trumps intercede for me?

On an island, in a high room,
On a kitchen table, by a chopping board

4

I set a book you once gave me, *The Travels of Mingliaotse*.
That ancient sage whispers in my ear:

*I have seen the sea changed three times
into a mulberry field and back again into the sea.*

COLD WEATHER TREES

Amma calls through the monsoon wind—
Come, Meena, pick up your sari hem
The snails mustn't catch in it,
If you go too slow into the next world
You'll stumble over a brawl of fireflies,
It is darker there than you imagine
Even the linden grove is filled with ghosts.
What does she know of cold weather trees?
She was raised by a pond where fireflies crawl
In a garden of jasmine and rain-bitten leaves.
Sometimes I feel everything's changed
In her moist house with its room full of mirrors
So I pick my way in through the cracks
To earth's sore place, navel of dirt
Under the cover of cold weather trees.

TORN GRASS

Childhood is a hot country, amma lives there.
The sky has turned the color of torn grass,

Think of the calf dragged away to Changanacheri Fair,
Tiny tottering thing, snout wet with gooseberry juice.

You crouched in the dirt, staring and staring,
Refused to come back in.

We had spiced pomfret, mangoes so ripe their sweat
Stained the damask tablecloth my dying mother left me.

Your grandfather's shadow hit the veranda.
He sat in his armchair, chewing on a cheroot.

Clouds swelled the mirror, broke its rosewood frame.
I saw your dead grandmother.

Look to your child! she cried.
I saw the mother cow, poor creature, her eye black,

Borderless, a lake you tried to drown in.
When ayah fished you out, your dress was soiled

With torn grass,
Your muslin petticoat so filthy I could not bear to touch it!

Remember how we sat on the veranda,
You and I, under a tinderbox sky,

Sun poking holes in the palmyra leaves,
Just like the summer your grandfather died,

When girls with umbrellas whispering catechisms
Passed by on the street, their petticoats billowing mist.

You recited some lines—
A child said what is grass?

A poem, wasn't it, about a child tearing up grass
With both her hands, fetching it to her mother?

IN KOCHI BY THE SEA

You walk in darkness,
A candle in your hand, your sari unravels,

An inch of cotton snatched underfoot,
Sheer wax catches the doorpost.

Amma, is something burning?
Anamnesis, I looked it up in the dictionary,

A seventeenth-century usage in the language
You helped me learn, of Greek provenance

Used by some in medical literature for signs
That help uncover bodily condition.

Who was she?
In Kochi, that sunbaked city by the sea,

I was high as your armpit.
You held me in your umbrella's shade.

We saw a woman very pale, squatting on a doorstep
"Rahel, Rahel!"

Someone was calling out her name.
A man, knife raised, circling a squawking bird.

The woman paid no heed.
The bird poked under her sari, disappeared.

In the shadow of her clothing in between her feet
We saw vermilion dots, a trickle, a slow pour.

She dipped one pointed finger, then another
In the show of blood

Making a flower, a fist,
A cockerel's head, a candle, a cloud,

A quickly changing river,
Parts of a city, many houses burning,

The sheaves of redemption reeling.
You drew me aside so sharply, shielded my eyes.

~

Anamnesis, I try to think
Of what Plato might have meant,

The body cleansed,
So seeing with the soul,

True recollection perfectly attuned
To every jot of what the future brings.

But there's a discomfort in the inner life
I had not bargained for—

A stream with blistered rocks where I must walk
Barefoot as I did so many years ago,

But now in a riverbed
Not marked on any map I learnt to read

In a schoolhouse with a palm tree outside
Where the barbarous sun pours.

~

When you dropped your candle
Nothing came to fire,

The future for an instant, pacified.
The dark was sweet and filled with singing birds

That fly into this garden without being asked,
A breath of joy, a fragrant certitude

Scarcely to be set into sentences.
Your umbrella was in the corner by the doorpost

Cupped in a flash of stormy light,
Its ribs bent and broken by that wind renewed,

A monsoon crossing the Arabian Sea.
And the woman we left behind?

Not to be seen except in figurations
Of the damned on Mattancheri palace walls.

There she squatted on a stony road
Making forms of blood—

Auguring what? Who could tell?
Figures cupped from the chaos of our dailiness,

Such ordinary things through which
We try to learn what the past presages,

And we think we touch
A clarity of longing, a blessedness.

~

The afternoon you dragged me from the street,
We walked beside the pounding beach

Past tiny wreaths of wood the color of wax
Washed out from the belly of a river,

Cast into shapes of ruined cities,
No-nation cities lacking anthem, flag,

Their lintels blown, gardens stilled into ash.
Torn free of you I ran into the wind.

Waves crashed into voices,
High-pitched, vulnerable,

The color of dropped blood,
The color of indigo cut from the mothering tree.

And underneath—in memory now—
I heard a darkness, luminous.

FOOD FOR MY MOTHER, ONE APRIL NIGHT

Snails on a black branch,
Sticky rice,
Burst morsels of light.

Under a stone arch
On white cloth, set cold figs, hot shrimps—
O fragrant night!

Outside the cook's hut
A stone, a sieve,
Butterflies in flight.

PALE BLOUSES

Rice blades in a muddy field,
Fretted gold bands fit for a dowry, tiny pearl-edged coffins.
So something else is wordless, as Chekhov might have said.

Amma is fearful her babies will be girls,
But she wants them to be the sisters she never had,
Three girls skipping in the graveled courtyard, tugging painted spools of
     thread.

Three sisters, as in the play she read, holding hands, longing to flee.
First sister melted her eyes into stones so no one could see,
Under her breath she sang songs of the monsoon wind.

Second sister trembled like a fox when its fur is stripped,
No one could bear the cadence of her cries.
Third sister took a strip of silk from grandmother's wedding sari,

Called out to the man in the crescent moon,
Sky Tailor come, it's time to set up your sewing machine on amma's
     veranda,
Time to snip the monsoon mist, stitch us pale blouses, help us make do.

LEMON TREE

Sister come second, amma almost died giving birth to you.
After you came, I scrambled out of the lemon tree.
I had hid there singing all year round and our parents loved me for it.

I watched through window glass
As the sky grew hot with desert gold, a heaviness blown south from
    Egypt.
A sun storm into which you leapt.

What did you think you were doing?
There was smoke in our room, your seersucker dress caught fire
And your seven dolls, even the one you called sweet Rosanna, started a
    meltdown.

Amma rushed from the kitchen, hands fresh from gutting fish.
On and on, she had to rub her wrists
In a bowl of cut lemons.

THREE SISTERS

We polished rosewood, folded up silks, shook out linens, she was
    coming home,
Second sister coming back at last.
Why linger at the bamboo root?

Stalks quake, a green break, a stake, hole hot at the heart's core.
Fishing flesh, a nook of tears.
Three sisters grew in a garden. Littlest sister sang: *High horse come get me!*

Born first I swore in my shoes to be mum.
Middle sister, crouching, cried as the wind hit the bamboo grove,
Thistle, thistle, come cover me!

BUDDHA OF BAMIAN

When he stares his eyes are several rooftops wide.
He is able to smell mauve petals of the winter orchid before they drop
    into snow,
Able to touch the carmine ribs of very old women,

Able to count each feather in the wings of wind-blasted eagles.
The Buddha of Bamian has no need of words.
Stone is his rod, and dripping water his staff.

Three sisters knelt at his feet praying for mercy.
Thou preparest a table before me, sang the oldest sister,
The younger sisters echoed her song, their words shatter in the desert
    storm.

FOUR FRIENDS

Makram, who loves the wild horses of Jebel Marra,
Tesir and Prakash—

Remember me, the girl with a scar on her knee,
The oldest of three sisters

Who fled a white house in Hai el Matar,
A girl who came to school too young and couldn't sleep?

At night I dreamt a sailboat on the Nile.
The boat caught fire, we perished together,

Four friends lost in that underworld pharaohs sought.
We reached for each other

Through the torn petals of our mother tongues.
Now my sorrow and my love smolder in a foreign language.

—I am she come from where I crave again to be—
Beatrice, girl who died too young,

I read those words thumbing through stacks of poetry
In a library by the Nile. The books have vanished

From the window ledge where I placed them a century ago.
Have they burnt the library?

Nostrils of the wild horses of Jebel Marra
Are filled with ash.

In a city where two rivers meet,
Makram, Prakash, Tesir, remember me.

SUMMERTIME

It was the hot season, fruit flies in bushes,
Mosquitoes on the porch boring
Through mesh, my straw hat buckling
Under packets of what looked like sea salt.
Plants suffering in moonlight.
It was far too bright, sky utterly cloudless
And bits of larkspur edged with stars.
The sea was all over,
Foamy, seamed with black where blunt
Rocks stood out in the bay.
Then someone came in a flat-bottomed boat
Saying a bomb had burst in Tavistock Square,
That a bus was on fire and, he added,
Perhaps it was safest to be on water.

POND AT GIVERNY

Out of the bushes comes a girl
In a boat and there is no noise in her.
She is ceremonious in a way
We are not used to anymore.
In her right hand is a net clipped
To a long pole and she uses it
To fish out leaves, twigs, and other
Impediments to the clear surface
Of the pond. Her movements are marks
On a clockface when time stops.
At her back a clump of water lilies
Someone planted well before her birth,
Sky colored, brushed indigo by water,
When touched by her net, fit to explode.

WATER GARDEN

Needing to live within the life of things,
He painted what he saw, water lilies rampant,
Rutting stalks the color of scarab claws,
Flung turquoise, iridescent opal
Cool as a rider guiding his horse's flank
Through clouds where the horse's head
Reappears, severed in a momentary mirror.
Something juts free, no ready shade discernible,
Blunt and raw and breathless.
Blind worm poking its head through filth.
Can form draw being, call it forth?
Breath skirts bone as you say to me:
May seems a good time to go to Giverny.
I'll come with you to Monet's water garden.

LAVINIA WRITES

See brother see! Note how she quotes the leaves.

—SHAKESPEARE, *TITUS ANDRONICUS*

In the museum, strip lining glowed in lamplight,
Droppings from the birds of Giverny
Stuck to scrolls once pinned in place
By shards of glass, skylights in a wartime studio—
Lines leached, paint blotted by his hands,
Throttle of breath, seesaw of passion.
1868 I think it was he tried to take his own life.
Two years and two decades after that he purchased land
And had them dig a water lily basin, ordered
A bridge be built to a shore no one else could see.

She holds up stumps where her wrists once were.
In her mouth, a stick guided with both her elbows,
So stooping writes the names of those who raped her.
The sky hangs clear in a water lily pond,
Paint refracting the feverish colors of her face,
Sole witness to his brushstrokes.
Late in sleep as eyesight turns to mist,
He watches windblown hair, bloody stumps.
Over and over he calls her name. In the trees,
Nightingales of Giverny unpick the thread of song.

MONET'S TROUSERS

In the garden, poppies and irises
Bled onto his shins and the cotton trousers
Alice had stitched for him got stained
At the cuffs with flowering colors so
He shuffled into the kitchen, thrust himself
Out of his clothes, and stood there utterly naked.
In the pewter bowl he saw himself, huge—
A monstrous thing. Then a woman so frail
He could barely make her out in all that summer
Sunlight got up out of her chair, picked up the soiled
Mess of cotton, stooped over the sink,
And started to wash it. Could it be her?
His body shook with terrible love
And he wept and wept facing death.

ALETHEIA (GIRL IN RIVER WATER)

First I saw your face,
Then your whole body lying still,
Hands jutting, eyelids shut,

Twin nostrils flare, sheer
Efflorescence when memory cannot speak—
A horde of body parts glistening.

Your feet were at an angle
Stuck in a tainted stream,
And under your ankles the specter of a horse,

Its chestnut mane lopped off,
An ordinary creature in a time of war,
Hooves blown, trying to make do.

PLAINSONG

I see a child in a bed, curls the color of coal,
Bones filled with fever, skin fit to smoke.

She makes a picture with stubby crayons,
With little sense of perspective,

Tincture of difficulty on ordinary paper.
A bird in a stream,

Soaking breast feathers, trapping water for its young,
But something stops the sandgrouse short.

Girl child and bird,
They tremble in the plainsong of dream.

~

Shall a fist wipe darkness
From exquisite portals that suck time in and blow it out?

Mother slips through a curtained door,
She has towels soaked in well water, to try to cool me down.

Does she feel the same blood beat in us both?
We were both victims of love.

~

I see a partition of rice paper and skin
Shaped like a bird's wing,

Fragile reparation enjoining us to sing,
And this is the tune that plays in my head

As I walk backward
Into a future that was never really mine—

"Something it was
That went and transfigured me."

But only the black keys give up their sound.
The ivories are still under construction.

TO ACHILLES

You were burnt all over by your mother,
Only an ankle remains, more raw than the rest of your skin.
She thought she was making you immortal.

I whisper this aloud, to you, Achilles,
Alphabets of ink too coarse to touch so fine a runner.
Do you recall the trill of the sandgrouse,

That fantailed bird, afloat in the deserts of Punt?
Your mother loved its wings,
Charred and lacquered into mirrors

To shield the faces of the dead.
Why did she do that to you?
Did she think you were a sandgrouse and could flit away?

Achilles, turn homeward now.
Let hunger pin you to her door,
Where a boy's foot is cast in ash.

VEIL

Amma's face is up close, she is tying my sash,
My dress is pink with tiny white spots,

Her eyes open wide as she stares at my thighs,
I tilt my face away, light strikes me.

Grandfather is strolling in the mulberry grove,
His walking stick covered in bits of torn grass.

Does amma see marks the color of burnt milk
Where grandfather hurt me?

Why does she shut her eyes?
I want us to be a mother and daughter

In someone else's poem.
How old was I?

Seven, at the rim of turning eight.
That season when mulberry bushes

Loosen their sleeves
And silk from grandmother's trousseau

Starts its slow pucker and float.
All through her wedding grandmother's face was veiled,

Silk from Varanasi the color of moonlight
—*Veiled with a special veil* . . .

Burned up in love and longing . . .
When grandmother died, she was wrapped

In her wedding sari so worms the color of milk
Could bite into her flesh.

How old was I when they laid grandfather
Down beside her in the muddy earth?

I cannot tell.
I tore skins from mulberry stalks using my teeth.

I refused to swallow the wet sour stuff.
Some things you never forget.

Three for Summer

Heaviness fell into things that had no weight
—OVID, *METAMORPHOSES*

1. NEELA MARYA

Sometimes things turn small and hard.
I like that, a pebble, I dug it out of the earth, lifted it up.

Hard white with streaks of blue inside.
The blue shifted around, swirling

As clouds do in the monsoon sky
Just before the rains start up and the air

Boils, spills into indigo. Lord Krishna's color.
Neela is blue in Malayalam.

Neela Marya I like to call myself.
If anyone calls, I will answer to that name.

I lift up the pebble, wipe the dirt off with my skirt.
I cradle the stone in my skirt, stare at it.

My skirt is rose-colored cotton. Fine cotton,
When the sun shines, you can see my legs.

My legs are solid flesh amma says,
So the sun can't shine through.

Amma makes me wear a petticoat.
It bunches up when I climb the guava tree.

I tear it with a guava branch.
I say, "Look amma, the tree did it!"

But she always gets me new petticoats.
White muslin, trimmed with lace.

"If I had Brussels lace I would trim your petticoats,"
Amma says. I know she loves me so.

Once I came in torn and wet,
The white petticoat between my knees.

I wanted to cry Jesus Lord turn me hard and cold,
A pebble with dirt on it,

That way no one will see through me.
As amma stared I felt my flesh melt

Into clouds, slow clouds in monsoon air
Just before the sun burns through.

2. WHAT AYAH SAYS

In dreams, the world is very small,
A pebble streaked with jet,

Flecks of carmine rush under its skin,
Held to the light it gleams as a jamun might,

Ruby pocked with indigo.
I splash my hands with well water,

Run my thumb over the pebble,
Hold it up to the sunlight.

I set it on my tongue,
Close my lips, and swallow hard.

Ayah says that when children
Swallow bits of bone,

Buttons, stones, they drop right out.
I wonder if the pebble will.

In front of the house, far from the toilet hole
Is the well filled with black water.

Everything rises from the well and ends up in it
Ayah says. Even girls I ask. Especially girls ayah says

Chewing hard on her clove. Ayah's back tooth hurts.
She chews cloves to keep the hurt from spilling.

When children swallow things they shouldn't,
They turn into stones, she says

They tumble into the toilet hole.
I squat on the toilet hole

The night owl cries so bright,
It perches in the leaves of the jackfruit tree.

Jackfruit is as big as a baby's head
With spikes on it, and pockmarks hot as lead,

If a jackfruit drops on your head
You will go to sleep, ayah said.

3 . DARK DOOR

A child went through a dark door into grandfather's library
The door was cut in jackfruit wood,

Varnished the color of burnt leaf.
Breath stops when I think of that door.

A child in a white dress walked in.
Later a child walked out.

Her eyes were burnt holes for the sun to shine through.
I do not like to say I.

She
Not I, not I!

What happened in grandfather's
Library makes me float.

No before, no after.
No up, down, down, up.

Who will save her?
Who will save Neela Marya?

She doesn't walk on water like Jesus or Gandhi,
She floats on it, eyes shut, bones poking through.

Will fishing nets turn parachutes, sail homeward?
Her dress was mussed up, wet.

Whose hand was on her thigh, wrist with hairs white
As the cabbage butterfly?

I held on to the kitchen door,
Amma! I cried, no sounds came out of my mouth,

I want to kneel inside your red sari,
Let the pleats swallow me.

Hand covered in a white towel, you stirred the pot,
It swarmed with sliced guavas, figs, mango pulp,

You trickled in crushed almonds, rosewater.
The towel over your phantom fist

Kept hot bubbles from hurting.
Amma, amma, noke, Nyan a, Nyan a, I cried,

Amma, look it's me, look I, amma, me!
But my lips were shut tight.

Later to keep me from floating,
I crouched by the well side, picked a tiny pebble,

Swallowed it. The pebble was the color
Of bright mist at monsoon time.

But clouds above the guava tree
Blew about so swift, it hurt to see.

I made my eyes huge:
I was a door the sun could pour through.

SONG OF THE RED EARTH

A child swings over laburnum and wisteria,
Over red earth covered in patches of grass

And frogs croaking in the gooseberry bush
And cisterns dripping water.

Torn grass makes a handkerchief,
Slow flag over a smoking abyss.

In the bone's hollows
The sparrow startles itself singing.

~

The child parts her lips to speak
And the sun is smeared with birth muck.

She loiters in a theater of cruelty,
Spoils of sense, ruin of syllables,

Iconostasis jammed with broken syntax
Where a royal door should be.

~

Decades later the woman writes:
I have no real home

And what is left of my childhood
Is fit to be carted away,

Remains of the dawn
In a spurt of circling wagons.

~

Gathering up bones, she listens for a child,
Dark child who dreams of catastrophe,

Who hears the turtledove on the sill,
The butterfly filled

With its own insuperable dust,
Hovering over springs of pure sulfur.

QUICKLY CHANGING RIVER

A woman in a striped sari checks out a list of names.
Hair bristling she stands in my way.

Meena floats away,
I have no stitch of sound to call my own,

Neither cotton nor silk cling to me.
I'm stuck in a thicket of passengers.

Who does she think she is, my given name,
Traipsing away like that?

A man approaches, from my father's side of the family.
His hair is filled with sand from Sinai's shore.

Look—my name has taken flight,
I'm milk splattered on dirt,

Salt on a cracked threshold,
A cloud in grandmother's well.

Can't you see? he replies,
She strolls in a forest of bruised tongues

Past bushes that burst into syllables.
She waits for you by a river that quickly changes color.

Deer drink there, the gold leopard,
Also speckled souls.

However long you wait, you'll
Never make the plane for Orange County.

For Rajen Harshe

TRAVEL TIME

To make the subject matter.
Is this a nightmare?
My luggage blown into air.

I race after it but cannot bump my self
High enough in heat to catch it.
The plane has flown, no shadows there.

My luggage hits the runway,
A mound of zippers and locks
Unhinged, raking sparks.

I hide behind a bush, see leaves
Burn in cold rotation, my baggage too,
Sheer melisma, ravenous ash.

NOMADIC TUTELAGE

You strike your head against a door
And pluck it back again, ancient gesture, ineluctable.

Bone bruising wood, and the lyric rears itself,
A silken hood.

Gamba Adisa, you have come to say,
Afraid is a country with no exit visas.

You taught me to fetch old meal for fire,
Sift through an ash heap, pick syllables, molten green,

Butting sentences askew.
I try to recall the color of your face.

Was it lighter than mine?
Was it the color of the East River

When the sun drops into soil
And I, a child by the well side, pack my mouth with stones?

So darkness crowns the waters
And the raw resurrection of flesh unsettles sight.

We would journey
Before light into a foreign tongue.

48

I hear you and I am older
Than moonlight swallows swim through.

Cries of hawks mark out four points of the compass,
Nomadic tutelage of cactus and rose.

Blunt rods strike blood,
Toss nets of dreams across salt shores.

In Memory of Audre Lorde, 1934–1992

Raw Meditations on Money

Things sold still have a soul. They are still followed around
by their former owner . . .

—MARCEL MAUSS, *THE GIFT*

1. SHE SPEAKS: A SCHOOLTEACHER FROM SOUTH INDIA

Portions of a mango tree the storm cut down,
a green blaze bent into mud
and they come to me, at dawn

three girls from Kanpur, far to the north admittedly
(we know this from national geography class,
the borders of states, the major cities).

They hung themselves from fans.
In the hot air they hung themselves
so that their father would not be forced to tender gold

he did not have, would not be forced
to work his fists to bone.
So that is how a portion of the story goes.

Slowly in the hot air they swung, three girls.
How old were they?
Of marriageable age certainly.

Sixteen, seventeen, and eighteen, something of that sort.
How do I feel about it?
What a question! I am one of three sisters,

most certainly I do not want father to proffer money
he does not have for my marriage.
Get a scooter, a refrigerator, a horde of utensils,

silks, and tiny glittering bits of gold
to hang about my ears and throat.
Gold is labor time accumulated . . . labor time defined.

Who said that? Yes, I am a schoolteacher, fifth standard
trained in Indian history and geography,
Kerala University, first class first.

The storm tree puts out its limbs and
I see three girls swinging. One of them is me.
Step back I tell myself.

Saumiya, step back. The whole history
of womankind is compacted here.
Open your umbrella, tuck your sari tight,

breathe into the strokes of catastrophe,
and let the school bus wait.
You will get to it soon enough and the small, hot faces.

See how the monsoon winds soar and shunt
tropic air into a house of souls,
a doorway stopped by clouds.

Set your feet into broken stones
and this red earth and pouring rain.
For us there is no exile.

2. HE SPEAKS: A FORMER SLAVE FROM SOUTHERN SUDAN

A fire, a flag, an earthen jug,
something white, something light
a cut hand waving.

He beat me with sticks, Abid, Abid!
Lie there in the dirt, in the den of black beasts.
Clean up after goats, camels.

Why do you not love me,
I asked, why beat me like this?
Because you are a slave, bought and sold for money.

∼

Hands were cut off, arms too,
as punishment for flight. Legs too.
For not cleaning the camels, for letting the horses loose.

Yes, I prayed to God.
God have mercy I prayed inside my soul
(the soul is a very silent place).

I had gone to sell beans my mother gave me,
eggs too, in the market in Nymlal,
a friend was with me,

twelve years old, tall as a reed.
He piped up when the raiders trapped us both,
they cut him in the throat.

A tiny girl knotted into a basket next to me
at the donkey's side
crying as a child must for mother.

The slaver wiped his sword.
Her neck a smashed jug,
the sun filled with blood.

A boy of seven, I saw this with my own eyes
and now I shut my eyes.
I want to see no more.

I have told my story
in churches also in the House of Congress.
I was a slave and many times I tried to flee bondage.

Now I go to night school,
study poetry—*the voices of slaves*
beneath the sun

and children bought with money.
I read all this in a language
the missionaries first taught me.

Each night she comes, my mother
kneeling at the swamp's edge,
both hands held out,

and I become a nothingness in air,
a homeless thing
a white flag fleeing.

My son, more precious than this, this,
she points to her flesh
her belly streaked with red mud, her breasts,

my son more precious than all the gold
heaped in the countinghouses of Upper Egypt.
May you shine under the blue dome of heaven.

⁓

O a fire, a flag, an earthen jug,
something white, something bright,
her cut hands waving.

3. SHE SPEAKS: A SEVENTY-FOUR-YEAR-OLD WOMAN TO HER DAUGHTER

By the Blue Nile, in your childhood
there was talk often of slavery.
People dragged from the south at gunpoint,

bought and sold for money in the markets of Kirio
and elsewhere; sometimes I tried to shut my ears.
We too were strangers, what could we do?

But it was an abomination, yes I use that word.
Human creatures bought and sold like beasts.
Under night skies I prayed for lost souls.

They had fled into the skies
and were staring down at me.
The stars were huge as burnt eyes.

In our own country no one wants girls as you well know.
Black money forces dowries up and
all those deaths by kerosene.

Why ask me these questions, child?
I cannot think straight anymore
about money and certainly if you tried

to live off your poems
you would starve like a desert sparrow.
Which is why we gave you a good education.

When I was a girl it was never spoken of.
Money was the unseen hand,
polishing mother's jade,

smoothing father's shawl,
raw silk he slung over the charka,
needing it when the cold winds bit the clouds.

Now Kanthama, who cuts the grass for me
under the mango trees, shivers in those winds.
I gave her the sweater you brought me once,

I hardly need it now.
She has sent her daughter
to Dubai so they can fix the roof of their shack,

put cement on mud floors, and so forth.
We grow older now.
We step into the garden for mangoes.

What we bring back is sunlight and loneliness.
The body is nothing but the spirit's house,
money has nothing to do with it.

But you tell me you can't afford to come from America
this summer. It is two whole years
since I saw you last. I feel my house is on fire.

CUTTING HAIR

I dreamt I cut your hair mama. It was scary.
My daughter laughs a little.
One bit of it hung over your ears and the rest of it was lower, didn't hang
    together.

She points with her pinkie, the varnish on it, black, peeling.
I hunch over the sink, rinsing out a mug, pour milk,
Set it in the innards of a microwave.

When I was her age, eleven going over the edge,
I felt silver scissors in my hands and around me,
Black hair flicked from the heads of womenfolk

Making a sea, a rocking thing, bloody water under stone steps.
And on and on the cutting went.
I trembled at the kitchen scissors amma hung on the rack,

The knife for gutting sandgrouse, chopping pigeon's wings.
My hands couldn't help themselves.
My daughter is weeping now.

I touch her cheek with my fingertips,
Stroke the sheen of fresh rinsed hair.
Pick the cup out of the microwave, watch her raise it to her lips, sip
    greedily.

Tiny noises are coming from her mouth, soothing us both.
Our animal selves not to be cast aside,
Understanding what we think of as our souls, setting us right.

ONCOMING TRAFFIC

Out of the bushes comes a boy, scarf round his throat
And rough mittens on his hands.

His hair is filled with sap from winter trees.
Through gates hung with orange flags he leaps

Through the second month of the year two thousand and five.
And the sea, miraculous, acidic,

Retreats, returning a wall of water, cloud driven,
Cumulative, gravity's portion

Where the child he was
Bobs up and down, seeing in sucked sky

A cumulus cloud the color of fire
And in the cloud, a man crying *I am your Lord!*

Now the fishes swallow darkness,
No one can net them

And sometimes they glint with gold.
Out of the bushes comes a boy

Whose bones have struck dissolving water lights
And tough stalks brushed with salt.

At the corner of Seventy-ninth and Central Park West
Stands a woman in a tan coat,

Head covered with a scarf.
She has a dog on a leash, a dog with long golden hair

And wet snout sniffing out death.
Seeing the boy, she cries out,

A sentence he tries to understand.
She lets loose her dog into oncoming traffic.

At the fiery Lord's command, she reaches out her hand,
Plucks the boy's beating heart, and, weeping, eats it.

For Frank Bidart

READING LEOPARDI

Late July, armpits of earth flung here and there,
Scent of shattered bark, clots of resin,
But this lime tree stands clear, shiny leaves bottling up heat.
I unwrap the scarf from my throat, I sit on a bench reading Leopardi.

Sempre caro mi fu quest'ermo colle
He begins and at the end
Longs to drown in dark infinity.
I'm three hundred miles from Recanati, his hometown.

Last night in a round of rushing wind,
I heard the names I was given flee from me.
Those names rose out of childhood and lagoon dirt,
Out of Arabic and wet sand,

Out of Hindi and fresh-pounded chili
Which amma always mixed with lime juice
When she came in from the garden,
A pile of fruit cradled in her sari.

Out of Malayalam and the milk of dreams
Scented with crushed almonds, my dead grandmother's recipe.
Out of the language of love, sharp moans
And low warbles, sweet muffled cries.

Stripped of the names that were given me, I sit silent in the shade
Of a lime tree reading Leopardi.
In a lake so deep it could swallow a hill I see stumps of wood float,
Making an altar of ruin, and slow waves turn the color of infinity.

HUNTING FOR FISH

A high-backed room above a canal becomes our gathering place,
Amma shrugs off a cotton blouse, unravels a six-yard sari.

Freed of ancestral plots of pepper and cardamom,
She is able to lift her knees and climb these wooden stairs.

My son, whose head just touches my belly button,
Bounds away, tugging a train made of matchboxes.

There are sparks on the bridge below,
Firecrackers perhaps?

My year-old daughter is gallivanting on her father's back,
They are hunting for fish in the open-air market.

He is my husband and for long lapses I have shifted myself
Against his blue waters and fled.

In another life I will sleep the long sleep with him.
Not here, not yet.

I am a housewife still, I have work to do.
The imagination presses against warm storage spaces,

Underground chalices for flesh.
I must open the bags my father packed before his last illness.

But why are we in this room only blackened stairs will reach
Above a canal of green blue water?

Underwater stones shift, our muscles knit,
Plucking strength to lift worn suitcases packed with family photographs.

Under sepia surfaces stir white ancestral bones
Still smarting in their skins of fat.

At the very end, we shall be cast—each soul in its morsel of flesh—
As bread on the shining waters of Venice.

HOUSE OF THE RED CANOE

Finally an address—2205 San Marco—
And a door inches from a canal where gondolas

Strut through green waters and opera singers put out to seed
Stand and moan "O sole mio" and other such things

And a woman with white hair, flesh shielded by a sari,
Sways beside a singer in his bulging shirt.

I stand on the sidewalk next to a red canoe,
It's propped against the dry wall, upended by fate.

The world has drifts and gristle sticking to stones
And rusty rivets stuck into underwater trees.

Njangal ivida! she cries in Malayalam,
My mother tongue, ancient language of the Dravidian coast.

Back against the wall I watch the ghost trees of Venice
Pick up their roots and approach me.

DOG DAYS OF SUMMER

In the dog days of summer as muslin curls on its own heat
And crickets cry in the black walnut tree

The wind lifts up my life
And sets it some distance from where it was.

Still Marco Polo Airport wore me out,
I slept in a plastic chair, took the water taxi.

Early, too early the voices of children
Mimicking the clatter in the Internet café

In Campo Santo Stefano in a place of black coffee
Bordellos of verse, bony accolades of joy,

Saint Stephen stooped over a cross,
A dog licking his heel, blood drops from a sign

By the church wall—*Anarchia è ordine*—
The refugee from Istria gathers up nails.

She will cobble together a gondola with bits of driftwood
Cast off the shores of the hunger-bitten Adriatic.

In wind off the lagoon,
A child hops in numbered squares, back and forth, back and forth,

Cap on his head, rhymes cool as bone in his mouth.
Whose child is he?

No one will answer me.
Voices from the music academy pour into sunlight

That strikes the malarial wealth of empire,
Dreams of an old man in terrible heat,

Hands bound with coarse cloth, tethered to a scaffold,
Still painting waves on the walls of the Palazzo Ducale.

SUN COLORED

In a café of yellow umbrellas my eyes fill with tears.
I listen to a girl dressed in black,

A student from the music academy.
She sings her heart out and mine in notes I cannot follow.

Under the wrought iron table, my feet are bare.
The stones of Santo Stefano hurt me.

She searches out a paradise of used colors,
Singing girl—woman I should say—

Her cap set out for a few lire
Boom box at her side.

Her voice scores the cobbles,
Stains the rim of my umbrella.

What would it be like to be born here?
I sip my glass of water and try to figure this out.

I feel as if Venice has been lying
In wait for me, all the days of my life.

What would it be like, I ask myself, to be born here,
To die within earshot of the suck and plop of canal water,

Floating sperm, laughter from hidden rooms?
A woman in a swelling dress turns,

Shadow thrust to a door—her child conceived in tumult—
Behind her, a stalk of lilies in his hand,

An angel, sun colored,
Imploring love to enter.

Self-Portrait in a Floating Mirror

Water equals time and provides beauty with its double.
—JOSEPH BRODSKY, *WATERMARK*

1

A cloud slips over a bristling field,
The wind sucks in colors so the cloud shows

Water through a ring of trees.
A bracelet of houses rises up and is glimpsed

By a man a woman and a child.
We shall live here, he sings

We, we, this family, us three!
And she, clutching a fan, an ivory caboodle

Threaded through with velvet ribbon,
Kicks up her shins and dances in bright motion

Over roots of starfish and mollusks
Sliced to make a clearing.

~

Decades later in an overcrowded house
He stretches on a cardboard couch, jots in a notebook

She will never see—*If I lived in Venice by the sea,*
Each morning would be ecstasy,

The inside of a cloud
As Tintoretto might have painted it.

And she, dressed in a cotton sari,
Blown through cloud cover, cries—

My pillow's thinning into blue,
the child has fled his coop, what shall I do?

In a swirling city at the water's edge
She opens up her purse,

Sets out her implements on bruised stone—
Glistening mirrors, pressed powder, lipstick.

She draws a house, mound shaped, precise,
Filled with the sweaty palms of children,

Her husband's thighs, his shirts stacked in a heap,
A house, rising as the moon burns

Into a cloud corolla where dead ones soar.
The Grand Canal flowers into mist.

~

Ancestral ghosts are clouding up her mirrors,
Doubling lips and thighs, shoots of wild mulberry

Slashed to make dye
For rotund hems, bulky silks for a marriage feast,

Tsunami of sleeves pouring into sight,
Heavenly wardrobe, costly metamorphosis.

Our earthly dwellings are ground into dirt.
Why are the groin of mango, necklace of tamarind,

And sweet-smelling champac foaming on rock?
She adds in poor Italian—*Campiello nuovo o dei morti!*

3

Venice of the floating portals,
Where mirrors hang in waters without foam

And the past is bled of all conviction,
Lost empire of salt and storm

I am seized by your dream of habitation
Scored by sun, your tongues warbling in seams of stone,

Crevices of cloud, balconies of bone,
In squares where clocks chime out in rhythmic gutturals

More musical than a cuckoo's lies.
Torn free of sense and circumstance,

Might I approach the darkness Tintoretto knew?
Turning to a palazzo door I trip

On fast furious brushstrokes—
Scrawl of the green element which mothers us.

ACQUA ALTA

Why come to Venice? the young woman asks.
I answer in lines—their time may have passed.

As a child, half a world away,
I floated in a black canoe, it sank in high water.

The lagoon swells at monsoon time and floods the Ghetto.
All the pepper of Muziris cannot buy their freedom or mine,

And painted pottery exchanged for monkeys
Or chattering peacocks cannot distill sorrow.

A fish with rainbow fins is swimming in a fountain,
It has swallowed the ring of remembrance.

This Kalidasa knew,
Dreaming of a high room by the Accademia bridge

That holds Sakuntala, still sleeping.
A bird, with feathers the color of jasmine,

Has made its nest in the timbers of that bridge.
There I see a man, face painted white,

A yellow star pinned to his chest,
Staring into water.

He too is part of this earthly theater.
No one must see him weeping.

VENETIAN PIGEONS

Instead of going to a Vivaldi concert, I stopped, waylaid by a pair of
    pigeons.
Like the couple hawking tickets for the concert

They too were in period costume,
No gold masks, or silver turbans, only feathers and claws.

I followed the pigeons up an alley by a shack of corrugated iron
Adorned with plastic bags puffed with garbage,

Red lights marking danger and the sign CALLE DEL CRISTO.
I pushed open a door to a worn-out palazzo.

Down the marble stairs strolled two men with a carpet,
A thing rolled up, with the figuration of palm trees,

Green and gold, giving off a stench.
The first, a masked man, whispered—

Touch it, go on, a chance for you.
The other, coughing—Mark—you know, the Evangelist?

And weren't you a child in Alexandria?
Upstairs—I am going, I replied.

To the Studio Dentistico of Prof. Dott. D. Vinanello Bote.
My friends have bought it, though hardly for a song and a dance.

So they're waltzing underwater?
The masked man kicked out his knee, the carpet sagged.

A hand tumbled out, flesh covered in salt with flecks of pork.
The body of Mark, for surely it was he,

Started to make signs no one could decipher,
Fingers and toes thrumming an intricate canzone

That summoned the pigeons, who swam in through the stairwell.
But all they had was a mess of pearly feathers

And beaks and claws
Struck dumb by the burden of heaven.

NO CEREMONY

Tintoretto made a toy house,
Set a boat on make-believe water,

Put spumes of smoke on a shifting floor
So no one could be sure

When a trapdoor would lift
And heaven pour through.

Under a darkened dome
The sun and moon have a rendezvous.

I met you in the piazza, your skin so bright
I thought the sun had burst through

The Pala d'Oro setting bones on fire.
I heard you say—

How could I belong to you
When all I have is cast afloat on water?

LOVE SONG WITH CRICKETS

It comes to me—
Mud lumped into balls, spittoons of sand,
Sortilege of crickets, festoons of them, strung over rocks,
Above the festive fires of Omdurman.

We were children then, knees, palms, thighs—
Crick, crack, crick, an old bicycle I had,
Past a wadi crammed with crickets, sticky antennae, iridescent wings
Flicking the sky into a violet blaze,

Casting the desert loose in us.
So pushing a wobbly bicycle,
Filled with longing we go,
On a road with nothing else to know.

WHITE NILE, LOVE SONG

Coarse sunlight, cotton shirt,
fistful of dates, bitten orange,
your sandals, my scarf.

Behind us
a room with a polished floor,
roses in extremis.

Will you love me after the end,
before the beginning,
by a stream of Nile water, bloodied by roses?

FLOATING ON FIFTH

Chairs upright, white tablecloth, glasses of Burgundy,
A street struck with light so things shimmer:

Pigeon wings, torn plastic bags.
Hands held out, a woman in a cloth coat drifts

Toward a lilac bush.
About her, singing starts, sounds pitched in an untoward clarity,

Noises so luminous they startle skin from bone.
I glimpse hairs on your wrist, the frayed seam of your sweater starts to
    bristle.

Under the table your knee bone kisses my knee bone
And I say somewhat loudly so you can hear me over the clatter

It could end, my life, poof like that, and it would be all right,
A turn of things, no more no less

On a street crisp with sun where a woman my age almost,
Coat torn, hair aflame, passes through lilac.

Where lads on bicycles flit as clouds do
Above Fifth, which is where we are,

Your eyes dark as everlasting and bicycle boys
With trays of seaweed soup and kimchi floating at knee level.

COMFORT STOP

We sat in a place they call a comfort stop,
Tepid coffee, piped music you found hard to bear,

We were meeting in a time of trouble, this much I knew.
Through soiled glass I saw a pool of asphalt, pile of cars, puckering sky.

Perhaps you and I will come together, I thought, or then again
Perhaps not. In the sky, clouds massed.

I saw sons crouched over fathers, seeking ruin.
Soldiers with blunt wires in their hands.

Men in hoods, others cut bare, still others fed through blackened tubes,
Prison dogs so quiet, their tails erect.

Who was it who wrote—
Absence of the imagination had itself to be imagined.

I brood on the great patience of the earth and how we turn away from it.
That afternoon, above the mound of cars, I saw birds—

Twin herons, wings out flung,
Fiery bouquet, feverish omen never to be stilled.

CLOSING THE KAMA SUTRA

In another country at the river's edge
We lay down in whispering dirt,
Then tried to fix a house with hot hope.
If we live together much longer
I'll become a cloud in my own soul.
Sweet jasmine floats in a bowl,
A keyboard harbors insects
(Mites in secret laying white eggs).
I must light frankincense to smoke them out
Else the alphabets will fail.
It is written in the *Kama Sutra*—
They embraced not caring about pain or injury,
All they wanted was to enter each other.
This is known as milk-and-water.

Love in the Afternoon

1

Late in the afternoon, two days running
The sky's a spindrift hole,

Backlit clouds hump into hills
Hovering over a sea of unwavering violet,

Waves mimic a house—
Host for memory,

Wild flag flung over nothing,
Nothing at all I can hold on to.

~

In a back room two children
Dreamt of by Dante:

She with hair drawn back,
Skirt crimson, moist with dew.

He, tender cheeked,
Palms a mourning dove

Fit to brush her lips.
In his pocket a bit of paper,

A calling card returned, sans address
Or watermark, utterly bare.

~

Two floating frames,
I see them stamped with indigo,

Petals of the dark lotus
Sporting a ring of nails

Sucked from a weaver's hands,
Set into bracelets of torture.

2

These are declensions of dream, merely
As coverlet damp with sweat

In our middle years we drop
Down, down, a deep down falling.

Will slit wrists hunger for skin?
Or cotton threads pulled

By finger and phantom thumb
Like nipples rubbed

Release a rare sweetness,
Surcease of sense?

~

In a house made of sand
A child with a pitcher at her hip

Goes down the veranda steps,
Her pale skirt blowing,

Her lips moist with voiceless syllables.
Who will pluck them into words?

Bold vernacular
That sings our bawling birth,

Our goings out and comings hither
Drawn into blessedness, a water crossing.

3

Late in the afternoon, two days running,
The botched and milky sky

Trailing behind,
I go down the subway steps.

In underground light I see
The face of a girl known to me,

Beatrice, child who swallows
Her own shadow,

Her short skirt cut of cotton
Seamed with silk

Stuck between her thighs
In the heat of an Indian summer.

~

Seeing her, the poet fainted.
A grown man fainting

On seeing a nine-year-old girl
Who has taken up residence in his memory.

What does this tell
Us about human nature?

~

When they picked him up,
His head shone with a cap of blood

As if the sky had torn a hole
To birth him.

And I heard him cry:
I am forced to write

Facing my love
For which no words exist.

OLD IVORY

Yesterday we spoke of tents, squat structures they coaxed us to,
 Needing that simple pleasure.

Why deny a lover a night or two close to the elements?
But each of us had turned away, whispering

—No, don't put me there—not wanting to touch
Crushed canvas, torn tarp, so close to burial soil.

We made a laughter of it then, voices pitched to sore jazz, razzmatazz
    reggae,
Making believe it was all alright, here in the middle of our lives,

Our goings-out and comings-in, scratches on bald rock,
Inaudible in the whisperings of slate, bits of bone, glacial dirt,

On this mid-Atlantic shore.
I try to imagine life in another country, our birth peninsula, broken in two.

Two women at Darah Sikhoh's wedding,
Necks craned to the crush of rose petals, faces veiled from sun,

Seated so quietly they might have been I and you,
Sister musicians painted in silhouette so fine

Only a magnifying glass reveals a fingernail
Haunting strings the tint of old ivory, irises stoked by light.

Behind the pair at the field's rim a tent soars.
An Englishman has set his shelter there.

Legs apart, hands awkward, he stands beckoning the women
As the sun slips back to the business of making light

And on the next page of a golden manuscript
Etched for a King of Kings

Darkness crawls over a sea of tents,
The body of love laid to ground, cadenza of lost belonging.

CADENZA

I watch your hands at the keyboard
Making music, one hand with a tiny jot,
A birthmark I think where finger bone
Joins palm, mark of the fish,
Living thing in search of a watering
Hole set in a walled garden,
Or in a field with all the fences torn:
Where I hear your father cry into the wind
That beats against stones in a small town
Where you were born; its cornfields
Skyward pointing, never sown, never
To be reaped, flagrant, immortal.

Three for Winter

1. AFTERNOON

I hear birds in the field
They are singing a long silence
It's a winter without guns.

Once I stood at the edge of the field
Where the trucks pass.
Perhaps you will come in the afternoon

When light is long and silence quickens.
What will love do to us?
No one can answer this.

2. TREES

I watch you in the distance
Strolling through winter trees
Some of which have fallen,

White pine and balsam
Toppling onto each other.
This has been going on for a long time.

Slow scrape of trees
Where water hardens,
Icicles snapping at the doorpost.

Sometimes it's as if I cannot see you.
Then love breaks me.
If I cry out, will you come to me?

3 . SKY

The gingko tree has a hollow trunk,
The snow around is blue.

Sometimes at night, moonlight
Leaks through.

How did we find each other,
You and I?

We make one creature with two wings,
Searching for the sky.

HOUSE OF BREATH

The threshold—running water—
I understood this early
And hot stones under the mango trees.

When I ran out to play
I had one house, then another and another.
Also the sea, where all roads finish.

I wandered at land's end
Feet veiled in mist.
Who can touch a gold horizon?

A bird sings in a garden
Made entirely of paper.
A brushstroke, a summit crossed.

I unpacked books, paper,
The burden of ink laid out
In the first house, which is also the last.

The stench of bodies heaped up
In the old city, the lorry with its canvas cover,
I was ten then, yes, that was it.

Mirrors burst from their frames
O the burnt skin of oxen!
In the shelter I ate flat wheat.

To get here, in late October,
I ran in rain, my heart beating hard.
Now I'm in a country that has no name.

Grief has no borders.
Past acres of barbed wire,
Damp stones, this house of breath.

Through ocher blossoms
A girl-child in flight.
Behind her, doors stopped with light.

The garden floats
And I search for my mother.
Dark rain, dream of us.

    For Zarina Hashmi

IMPRINT OF MEMORY

The curtains made of mulmul started fraying.
So too the weave of longing.

We are all bound with threads of longing.
I laid her in her grave.

Yes I was there, a spirit hovering,
At least that's the way I see it now.

It's hard to say what happened to my body.
I saw trees, five of them.

They held up light in their branches
Almost like a mirror—

The imprint of memory
Cast back from the place where it occurred

As if to calm by repetition,
Which is the other side of the wound.

There are five trees in paradise,
It is written in the Gnostics.

And the leaves on those trees turn green,
And never fall.

AUGUST 14, 2004

I have never been to Kraków,
I imagine it filled with chestnut trees.

It was a green day when you died and hard the telling of it,
Now is the time for patience.

The west is a knot of thundershowers,
The east, a nest of small-scale fires.

On terraces covered with roses
Instead of honeybees, bullets swarm.

In alleyways torn silk reveals the bodies of infants
Laid head to toe in caskets of desire.

On a dresser made of mahogany
A woman's hand arranges a display of attar,

Each vial culled from a separate continent—
Jasmine, lilac, rose—last of all, attar of earth,

Red earth in pouring rain,
August 14 in the year of the Lord 2004.

Was it wet in Kraków when you died?
Through airport lounges and shuttered doors,

Through coastlines gashed by mist
Through barricades of blunt words,

Torment of the ant and ox,
In a miserable century with its corrupt couplings

You kept note of it all,
Petticoats trimmed with lace from the black heart of Europe,

Cotton from India, crystal from Lithuania,
A woman's cheek wet with dew as paradise swims up,

Gold fish, icon of the journeying soul,
In a garden pond struck by muscular roots and fleshly scents,

Ferocious toil with pitchfork and spade.
How much time is enough in the life of a poet?

You cannot answer now.
The chestnut trees are thick with rain.

You turn away from the windowpane,
The dirt is a honeycomb of consonants.

Hour by hour as you come close to your death
Someone whose face is covered with a veil,

Man or woman I cannot tell,
Reads from the Letter of Paul to the Corinthians.

Reads in a slow, clear but quavering voice,
In speech that erodes the clarity of your own,

Crystalline disturbance of the liquid atmosphere
Where sun and storm collide,

Reads in the tongues of men and of angels
From the poems you composed and poems to come,

Zone of limestone, chestnut, and linden
Zone of sweet water, laced by fever,

Book of the migrant soul,
Now losing, now finding love.

In memory of Czeslaw Milosz, 1911–2004

Acknowledgments

Some of the poems in this book first appeared in the following publications; my thanks to the editors:

American Poet: "Love in the Afternoon"

Atlas: "Three for Winter," "Quickly Changing River," "Food for My Mother, One April Night"

Ars Interpres (Sweden): "In Kochi by the Sea"

Barrow Street Review: "Self-Portrait in a Floating Mirror"

Black Renaissance/Renaissance Noir: "Cosmopolitan," "Love Song with Crickets," "White Nile, Love Song"

Drunken Boat: "Reading Leopardi," "House of the Red Canoe," "No Ceremony"

Harvard Review: "Dog Days of Summer," "Closing the *Kama Sutra*," "August 14, 2004," "Acqua Alta"

Kavya Bharati: "Transit Lounge" (earlier version of "Quickly Changing River")

Kenyon Review: "Cold Weather Trees," "Torn Grass"

Lake Effect: A Journal of the Literary Arts: "Floating on Fifth"

Literary Imagination: "Summertime"

Massachusetts Review: "Song of the Red Earth"

South Asian Review: "Old Ivory"

Little Magazine: "Lavinia Writes"

TriQuarterly: "Pale Blouses," "Plainsong"

Washington Square Review: "Aletheia (Girl in River Water)"

Women's Review of Books: "Raw Meditations on Money"

Women's Studies Quarterly: "Nomadic Tutelage"
World Literature Today: "Four Friends," "Comfort Stop"

∽

"In Kochi by the Sea" appeared in *White Ink: Poems on Mothers and Motherhood*
    (Toronto: Demeter Press, 2007).
"Aletheia (Girl in River Water)" appeared in *Monika Weiss: Five Rivers* (New
    York: Lehman College Art Gallery/Editions Samuel Lallouz, 2007).
"Hunting for Fish" appeared in *Transformations in Contemporary Indian Families:
    Reading Literary and Cultural Texts*, eds. Sanjukta Dasgupta and Malashri
    Lal (New Delhi: Sage Publications, 2007).
"House of Breath" appeared in *Zarina: Weaving Memory, 1990–2006*
    (Mumbai: Bodhi Art, 2007).

∽

My gratitude to the Fulbright Foundation for the Senior Specialist Award
that allowed me to travel to Venice; to the Presidential Travel Fund of
Hunter College for a travel grant to India; to the Corporation of Yaddo for
the award of the Martha Walsh Pulver Residency for a Poet—a time of
grace in the cold of a Saratoga winter when I was able to compose several
of these poems.

∽

My love and thanks to David Lelyveld, Adam Kuruvilla, and Svati Mariam,
who lived with me through the writing of this book; to my sisters, Anna in
Tiruvella and Elsa in Chennai; to friends who listened to the poems, read
them in disparate versions, offered comments on drafts of the manuscript—
Frank Bidart, Marilyn Hacker, Domna Stanton, Zarina Hashmi, Andrea
Belag, Sudeep Sen, Shaul Bassi, Andrea Sirotti, Daniel Brewbaker, Chris
Hobson, Erika Duncan, Karen Malpede, Kazim Ali, Ronaldo Wilson,
Monika Weiss; to Gauri Viswanathan, Rajen Harshe, Svati Joshi for lifelong
friendships on two separate continents, sustaining me.

Notes

"Cosmopolitan": The poem is addressed to Chan Kwok Bun who in Pandan Valley, Singapore, asked me to write a poem on cosmopolitanism.

"Torn Grass": The quotation in the last line of the penultimate stanza is from Walt Whitman's "Song of Myself"—one word missed.

"Four Friends": Jebel Marra is the mountainous region of Darfur, in the west of Sudan.

"Alethia (Girl in River Water)": Composed after seeing the performance "Lethe Room" by Monika Weiss. December 13, 2005, New York City, Lehman College Art Gallery.

"Veil": The words in italics are from the Sufi poet Faridudin Attar (c.1230 C.E.) evoking the most celebrated of the Sufi women mystics, Rabi'a al Adawiyya (c. 801 C.E.), also known as Rabi'a of Basra.

"Dark Door": This last section of the three-part poem "Three for Summer" retraces some of the same ground as "Book of Childhood," a chapter in my memoir, *Fault Lines* (2003, expanded version). I worked on the poem, it remained in draft form as I wrote the prose, published it, turning then to the poem that in fact came first for me.

"Raw Meditations on Money": The epigram is from Marcel Mauss, *The Gift: The Form and Reason for Exchange in Archaic Societies*, trans. W. D. Halls (New York: Norton, 1990), p. 66. The line in italics in the first section comes from Karl Marx, *Grundrisse: Introduction to the Critique of Political Economy*, trans. Martin Nicolaus (New York: Vintage, 1973), p. 134. The second section "He Speaks: A Former Slave from Southern Sudan" draws on the words and testimony of Francis Bok. I heard him speak in New York City in the year 2000. Bok is the author of *Escape from Slavery:*

The True Story of My Ten Years in Captivity and My Journey to Freedom (New York: St. Martin's Press, 2003). The lines in italics in this section come from William Blake, "Visions of the Daughters of Albion" *The Complete Poetry and Prose of William Blake*, ed. David Erdman (New York: Anchor Books, 1988), p. 46

"Nomadic Tutelage": In memory of Audre Lorde, 1934–1992. In 1987, when I joined Hunter College, Audre had the office next to mine. She was a friend and mentor to me. The lines in italics are from Audre Lorde, *Our Dead Behind Us* (1986): "Diaspora" and "From the Cave" (*The Collected Poems of Audre Lorde* [New York: W. W. Norton and Company, 1997], pp. 383, 389).

"Oncoming Traffic": The orange flags were hung in the winter of 2005 by Christo and Jean Claude for their Gates Project, Central Park, New York City, 1979–2005. Frank Bidart's poem "Love Incarnate" led me to the passage: "I seemed to see a cloud the color of fire in my room and in that cloud a lordly man. In one of his hands he held a fiery object: 'Behold your heart! . . .' He awoke the sleeping one and through the power of his art made her eat this burning object in his hand." Dante, *Vita Nuova* (chapter 3). Frank Bidart, *Desire*, "Love Incarnate" (New York: Farrar, Strauss, and Giroux, 1999), p. 5. Dante Alighieri, *Vita Nuova*, trans. Mark Musa (New York: Oxford University Press, 1992), p. 6. The word "master" is used by Musa in his translation, but I prefer to follow Bidart, who uses the word "lord."

"Reading Leopardi": *"Sempre caro mi fu quest'ermo colle"* (I've always loved this lonely hill) is how Leopardi begins his 1819 poem "L'Infinito."

"House of the Red Canoe": Dedicated to Shaul Bassi and Suzie Franco. Shaul first invited me to Venice and in Shaul and Suzie's home, 2205 San Marco, several of these poems were composed.

"Comfort Stop": The line in italics in stanza 6 comes from Wallace Stevens's poem "The Plain Sense of Things": "Yet the absence of the imagination had / Itself to be imagined." Wallace Stevens, *Collected Poetry and Prose* (New York: Library of America, 1997), p. 428.

"House of Breath": This was composed at the request of my friend and fellow traveler Zarina Hashmi, whose art has meant so much to me. The poem evokes her set of fourteen portfolios of works on paper, first exhibited in Bombay at Bodhi Arts in 2007.

"Imprint of Memory": The Gospel of Thomas 19: "For there are five trees in Paradise for you; they do not change summer or winter and their leaves do not fall." (Q *Thomas Reader,* eds. Kloppenborg et al. [Sonoma, Calif.: Polebridge Press, 1980], p. 134). Composed at Yaddo, October 10 to November 25, 2005.

ABOUT THE AUTHOR

Meena Alexander, Distinguished Professor of English at Hunter College and the Graduate Center of the City University of New York, is the author of several books of poetry, most recently *Raw Silk* and *Illiterate Heart,* winner of a 2002 PEN Open Book Award. Her memoir, *Fault Lines,* was one of *Publishers Weekly*'s Best Books of 1993, and her novel *Nampally Road* was a 1991 *Voice Literary Supplement* Editor's Choice.